D1577857

Sedona's Best Vortex Guidebook

Experience the Magic of Sedona's Sacred Energy Centers

Jamie Jones

My Imagination
Sedona, Arizona

© 2002 Jamie Jones

Published and distributed in the United States by:

My Imagination, 2260 Roadrunner Road, Sedona, AZ 86336
Phone (928) 204-2214, Fax (928) 204-1399
email: ideas@my-imagination.com

Cover Design & Typesetting
My Imagination
Sedona, Arizona

Photography by Bob Bradshaw

All rights reserved. No part of this book may be reproduced by any mechanical, photographic, or electronic process, or in the form of phonographic recordings, nor may it be stored in a retrieval system, transmitted, or otherwise be copied for public or private use—other than for "fair use" as brief quotations embodied in articles and reviews without prior written permission of the publisher.

Library of Congress Control Number: 2001 135568
ISBN 1-886966-18-4

Printed in United States of America
0 9 8 7 6 5 4 3 2 1

First Edition: In Print Publishing, January 2002
Second Edition: My Imagination, July 2007

THIS BOOK IS DEDICATED

to

My sons, Brayden and Ethan
and my daughter Emerson

...the greatest blessings in my life.

Acknowledgment

I would like to thank Anita Dalton
and Tomi Keitlen for sharing,
so unselfishly, their experiences,
wisdom, and support during the
creation of this book.

Contents

Introduction

When the author of this splendid guidebook, Jamie Jones, asked me if I would allow her to use the Prologue of my new book, "Beyond My Fear," I thought and thought about it. I finally said *yes* as it depicts an experience that led to more healing of my, then, physical problems.

Beyond My Fear

November 30, 1987

It was as if a magnetic force was pulling me forward, propelling me, dragging me, and tugging at me. I was bewildered, almost disoriented as I could not understand what was happening to me.

Suddenly a voice, an authoritative, faceless voice from inside my head demanded, "Tomi, this is Bell Rock. Pull your car off the road and turn off the ignition."

Momentarily, I considered that what I had heard was not of this world. It was strange and alarming. I thought I had to be suffering from some sort of delusion. Defiantly, I shook my head from left to right, and back and forth again. I shouted, "No, damn it! Why should I? I am in control of me. No outside forces can tell me what to do!"

For so long, things had happened to me that I could not control—blindness, illness, and the loss of loved ones. I had to exert control over my own life from such forces and I wasn't about to surrender to anything resembling them again.

But the words were calmly reiterated, "Tomi, you're at Bell Rock. Pull off the road and turn off the ignition."

This time my mind's core accepted the voice; there was a frightening tinge of recognition that slowly began to entertain some reason. I shook my head again but this time in acquiescence.

I knew without a doubt that I was at Bell Rock, one of the vortices in Sedona, Arizona where I had been living for five weeks. My living room, by conscious design, faced Bell Rock offering me a view of such grandeur, of such superb mystical magnetism that it brought a beatific peace. I knew and had experienced the sacred resonances that surrounded the entire Red Rock area and all the vortex energy that had lured me there. Bell Rock, in particular, was now a part of me and was very much the ingredient that called me to this small, sacred corner of the earth.

Intuitively, I understood that I **had** to somehow climb the bell-shaped rock. Yes, it was imperative. I had to. An inner knowing told me that I absolutely had to climb, if not to the summit, then at least partway.

I parked the car, reached in the back seat for the two canes that enabled me to walk short distances. How I was going to ascend the rocks was an enigma to me since, for four years, I had been unable to maneuver more than a block or two at a time. Yet, I held my canes firmly and stood tall and erect. Step by each labored step, I began to negotiate the wide rocky plateaus. With each step I sensed an excited determination and more strength than I had been able to muster during the long period off my illness. Something, or someone, was supporting my every move. Climb I did.

While reaching the pinnacle was impossible, I somehow, miraculously managed to ascend at least one-third of the way up the Bell. Then that same inner knowing led me to a flat stool-like rock where I was able to lower my body to rest and reflect upon the exhilaration that was mine. I was flooded with a wild, intense pleasure. There was such extraordinary, awesome comeliness all about me that it brought tears to my eyes, while giving me intense pleasure. The beauty was drawing me right to its epicenter—directly to its very heart. The energies were so powerful, I was lifted up to a dimension that was totally unfamiliar to me. Yet I recall crying out, "This is where I will be helped. This is where I will be healed. I know it. I just know it!"

Quietly, as I sat in reflective, meditative silence, an image appeared before me so real that I felt I could reach out and touch it. I focused harder, blinking my eyes to help it take shape. Intangible, immaterial, yet it appeared to be—yes, it was! It was my David. It was, and yet it couldn't be. It was impossible. My David had been killed in a head-on collision years ago. But it was David!

"David, David," I cried, reaching out to him, wanting to touch his hand—to feel his warmth again. His never-forgotten voice spoke: "My dearest Tomi, it has been such a long time. It is all right. I am here with you now and we will be together always. Dearest Beloved, you are finally on the right path. I have waited, oh so long, for you to find your way back to me. The teacher you need will soon be with you. I shall stay by your side with my love and whatever guidance you may need. Nothing can hold you back, Dear One. Nothing.

With these few words, the vision of my David gradually faded from sight. Crying, I reached out to him, but once again he was no longer of this world. At least, not at that time.

TOMI KEITLEN

Author of "Farewell to Fear"
published by Bernard Geis Associates

"Beyond My Fear" to be published
by In Print Publishing in 2002

After you have read the Introduction, know that I did find a wonderful teacher, in fact, three very wonderful teachers. They were La Mer Marshand, Magdalena, and Marty Wolf.

I continue to have many close experiences with my twin soul David. At 80 years of age, I still frequent Bell Rock and find love, peace, energy and great joy.

Palatki Ruins

Foreword

With its towering crimson spires and remarkable natural beauty, Sedona has become a world famous destination for travelers around the globe. Founded in 1902, Sedona was named for Sedona Schnebly, the wife of the first postmaster in this area.

Nestled amongst pristine forest land and majestic red rocks, this popular town has become known for much more than its breathtaking scenery. Sedona has become known as one of the most powerful spiritual centers on earth. This power reaches beyond the awesome landscape to the major power points that exist here, known as the Vortex Sites. Sedona has become famous for having such a large number of vortices in such a concentrated area and its popularity has increased immensely in the past decade.

These vortices are various locations in nature where vital energy is emitted in great abundance. The vortex centers have an aliveness and intensity of life-force energy that is amplified and concentrated. This spiraling energy flowing from the earth has been documented by human experience over the years and has been responsible for spontaneous healings and spiritual awakenings for hundreds of people. You will find several testimonials of these magical vortex experiences beginning on page 50.

You can sit around and wait for science to finally prove that the vortices exist and can be measured with modern technology, or you can hike up to nearest vortex site and experience this amazing energy for yourself.

One of the most common questions travelers have asked is, "How does this energy affect me?" The answer to that question is that the energy of the vortex will amplify anything you bring to it. For example, if you bring the desire to increase your intuition, it can help to open that awareness. If you arrive at the Vortex with addictions or emotional traumas, the energy will usually bring those things to the surface to help you release them more quickly. Others find that physical ailments and pain may be released rather suddenly. It all depends on the individual and their willingness to be open to receive the healing effects and magic of these powerful places. For some who remain closed and skeptical, the healing will not be received or may simply intensify their resistance to healing and moving forward.

While traditional scientific measures of this energy are few, we cannot disregard the hundreds of miracles and magical healing experiences that have been discussed and shared by seekers throughout the years.

Remember, the best proof you can gather is to experience the energy yourself. Whether your intent is to heal and spiritually rejuvenate, to access your psychic abilities, or to feel more inspired, the beauty and powerful energy of Sedona can be the perfect facilitator for you.

The seven major vortices of Sedona are featured in the upcoming text of this book. Some will involve light hiking or walking to reach, while others can be easily accessed by car. Before you begin your vortex journey you will need to purchase a Red Rock Pass which is required for vehicle parking on the National Forest in Red Rock Country. The Red Rock Pass Program is designed as a conservation tool to help preserve the natural beauty of Sedona so our children will be able to enjoy this amazing landscape for years to come.

Red Rock Passes are available at the locations listed below for the following fees:

| $ 5 | Daily Pass | $ 20 | Annual Pass |
| $ 15 | Weekly Pass | $ 40 | Grand Annual Pass |

Red Rock Passes can be purchased at the Sedona Chamber of Commerce in Uptown Sedona or at one of the three "gateway visitor centers" listed below:

North Gateway: Located on Highway 89A at the Oak Creek Vista Overlook at the top of Oak Creek Canyon.

South Gateway: Located on Highway 179 at the Tequa Plaza in the Village of Oak Creek located 7 miles north of the I-17 exit.

West Gateway: Located on Highway 89A at the Sedona Cultural Park in West Sedona just 1 mile past Dry Creek Road.

Map for the Gateway Visitor Centers

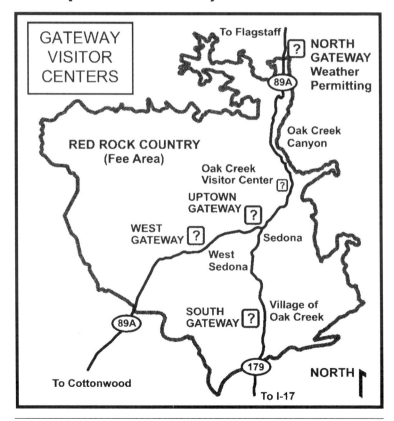

Safety Guidelines for Vortex Travelers

A SAFETY MESSAGE FOR ALL VORTEX TRAVELERS

Before you embark on your spiritual adventure through the vortices of Sedona it is important that you follow some important guidelines to ensure a safe and happy journey.

1. Please be sure to wear the proper footwear for walking or hiking such as hiking boots or athletic shoes with good tread on the bottom to prevent slipping.

2. Make sure you have plenty of bottled water with you, as the dry heat and altitude of this area can dehydrate you quickly.

3. It is wise to stick to the marked trails and stay with your group so no one is lost and your car is easily found at the end of your day.

4. Nutrition bars or other energy snacks such as trail mix or fruit will help you to make it to your destination with much more energy and stable blood sugar levels. Remember, food is fuel and your body will run much longer on a full tank.

5. Start out early enough in the day on your hike when there is still plenty of sunlight left. You do not want to start out at 5:00 pm for a three hour hike and wind up in the dark unable to find your way back. Do bring a flashlight just in case.

6. Sunscreen and a hat are highly recommended due to the intensity of the Arizona sun.

7. Keep your eyes forward and on the trail as other inhabitants of the areas such as snakes and Javelina have been known to appear. As long as you stay on the trails you should be okay. Remember you are in nature's house and should take precautions to make sure EVERYONE, including the wildlife, is safe.

Airport Mesa Vortex

With one of the best sunset views in all of Sedona, this vortex site emits a subtle "electric" energy that recharges the physical body and aids in opening our body's energy centers, known as the "chakras." The energy here is best used for enhancing psychic abilities and expanding one's consciousness, but can also be used to increase physical energy.

For those looking to increase their spiritual and intuitive abilities, you may want to carry an amethyst crystal in your pocket to further increase the energy of this site.

Airport Mesa offers fantastic views and is easily accessible by car. I highly recommend exploring the trails in this area and finding a quiet space to sit and breathe in the positive and uplifting energy. While there is an uphill trail leading off to the left, there is also an outlook where you can park and still experience the energy of this vortex.

Airport Road

✧ _____ ✧

HOW TO GET TO AIRPORT MESA

From the "Y" intersection of Hwy 89A and Hwy 179, go 1.1 miles west on 89A and turn left when you reach Airport Road. Proceed up the road about a half mile to the parking area on the left. You can walk up the trail directly ahead of you between the two hills. This entire area is the vortex site, so feel free to wander to your own private space where you can sit and relax or meditate. One of the most spectacular times to visit Airport Mesa is at sunset. The views are incredible and the energy is rejuvenating and inspirational. However, it can get quite crowded around this time so if you wish to avoid the congestion, it is best to go early in the morning or around lunchtime when most other travelers descend to the local restaurants for a bite to eat.

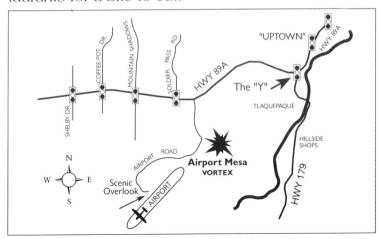

Cathedral Rock Vortex

This awe-inspiring vortex is also one of the most photographed. Its orange towering spires and buttes rise up from the earth with amazing beauty and power. While the appearance of this vortex is strength and force, it actually provides one of the most calming and soothing energies of the area. The natural beauty of the red rock country mixed with the flowing waters of Oak Creek makes this setting perfect for splashing in the creek or sitting quietly in reflection and meditation.

The energy of this area helps one to relax and rejuvenate with a feeling of serenity that soothes the soul. The tranquil natural surroundings and the life-giving waters of the creek emit some of the most calming energies in Sedona. For this reason, Cathedral Rock, also known as Red Rock Crossing, is the perfect place for stress reduction, regeneration of the physical body and rejuvenation of one's spirit.

Once at this site, you will experience a separation from the hustle and bustle of the outside world and enter a universe where you are at one with nature. In this space where nothing else seems to exist but

Cathedral Rock

the whispering breezes of the wind and trees, you can experience some of the most powerful meditations in all of the world.

HOW TO GET TO CATHEDRAL ROCK

The easiest way to access Cathedral Rock is to drive 4.5 miles west on 89A from the junction of Hwys 89A and 179 until you reach Upper Red Rock Loop Road. Turn left and drive 1.8 miles to Chavez Ranch Rd. Turn left and follow the pavement .8 mile and turn left into Crescent Moon Park. Drive as far into the park as possible and then walk to the creek. As you walk along the creek, head towards the base of Cathedral Rock where the energy is the strongest.

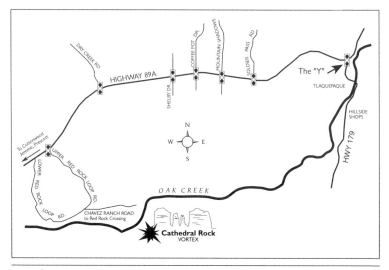

Bell Rock Vortex

ne of the most visible vortex sites off Hwy 179 as you enter Sedona from the Village of Oak Creek is Bell Rock. This amazing natural creation of red rock in the shape of a bell is one of the most popular and sometimes crowded energy centers in all of Sedona.

Upon seeing Bell Rock for the first time, an overwhelming feeling of wanting to jump out of your car and run up to play on this unique rock formation may come over you. Please carefully pull over and park your car before doing so.

The "electric" energy of this site has been called the "activator" due to the intensity of the energy. This vortex will rejuvenate and increase your physical vitality and energy. It also appears to bring out a playful childlike energy in some that helps to release and free the inhibitions of our more serious adult self. Many travelers to this site have experienced profound, and sometimes spontaneous, physical healings.

Bell Rock ✧_____✧

HOW TO GET TO BELL ROCK VORTEX

Bell Rock is on Hwy 179, just north of the Village of Oak Creek. If you are coming from Sedona, this vortex is just 5 miles south of the junction of Hwy 89A and Hwy 179 (at the "Y"). There are several turnouts where you may easily park your car in front or near the site. There is also an area south of Bell Rock where you can park. Several clearly visible trailheads will lead you directly to the base of Bell Rock.

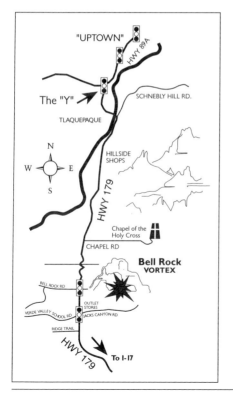

Chapel Of The Holy Cross Vortex

Built in 1956 by Marguerite Brunwig Staude, this impressive modern structure stands tall between two natural red rock pinnacles. This is my personal favorite vortex in Sedona, best experienced when you enter the sanctuary of the Chapel itself.

The energy of this location is one of the strongest and most easily felt in all of Sedona. The feeling within the walls of the chapel is one of inspiration and joy. The energy of this site also includes love, harmony, unity, and oneness with all that is.

The first time that I experienced the Chapel for myself and entered this sacred sanctuary, I burst into tears of gratitude and joy as I was instantly filled with intense feelings of unconditional love and acceptance. Others have described feelings of inspiration, awe and renewal upon entering this holy site. What magical journey awaits at the Chapel of the Holy Cross? Visit today and see for yourself. Be sure to light a candle at the altar and leave your blessing or prayer.

Chapel of
the Holy Cross

HOW TO GET TO
THE CHAPEL OF THE HOLY CROSS

From the "y" intersection in Sedona, head south on 179 about 3 miles until you reach Chapel Road. Turn left and follow this winding road directly up to the parking lot of the Chapel where you will find plenty of parking.

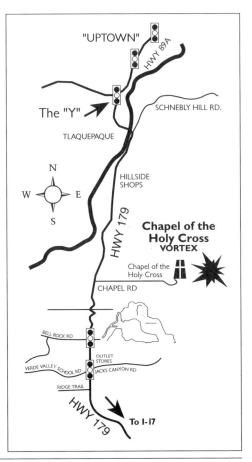

Schnebly Hill Vortex

The rough terrain of the road leading up to the top of this vortex site can be exciting for the adventurous at heart. This partially paved and partially dirt road passage leads up to one of the highest plateaus in Sedona where the views of Sedona and Oak Creek Canyon are amazing.

The energy at this site is cleansing and purifying. For those who are looking to release old negative patterns and blockages, this is the place! Remember that all vortices emit energy and for those who just wish to feel increased energy and vitality, Schnebly Hill will also do the trick.

Schnebly Hill

HOW TO GET TO SCHNEBLY HILL

From the "Y" intersection in Sedona, drive south on Hwy 179 for half a mile. Once you cross over a small bridge, turn left onto Schnebly Hill Road. This road will turn to dirt after a mile but will continue up to the vista at the top of the hill where you will be able to pull off and park.

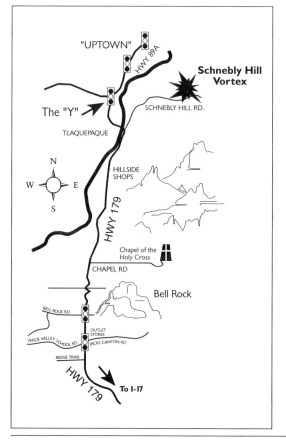

Boynton Canyon Vortex

This canyon is full of vortices though it is listed as only one vortex on most maps. The area of Boynton Canyon is vast, with dozens of scenic windy trails and mesas for your exploration.

It is best if you set aside an entire day for the exploration of this site. Once you enter this magnificent canyon you will be seduced by the rugged natural beauty of the unique terrain and may lose track of time and the world you left behind.

This magical and vast canyon encompasses both masculine and feminine energies and is ideal for balancing these energies within oneself and for harmonizing relationships with others—whether business or personal. Hikers of Boynton Canyon have also described a renewed sense of purpose and direction in their lives and the motivation to move forward in pursuit of their dreams.

Boynton Canyon

✧ ———————————————————— ✧

HOW TO GET TO BOYNTON CANYON

From the "Y" intersection in Sedona, drive 3.2 miles west on Hwy 89A and turn right when you come to Dry Creek Road. Follow this road until you see signs directing you to Boynton Canyon. If you end up at the entrance to Enchantment Resort, turn around and go back 220 yards to the parking area. From this parking area, walk along the trail marked Boynton Canyon Trail No. 47. This trail will take you to a powerful vortex location. Remember, the canyon is full of trails that lead to intense energy centers so do not be afraid to explore the area freely. However, for the safest day of hiking, remain on the main trailheads and carry plenty of water.

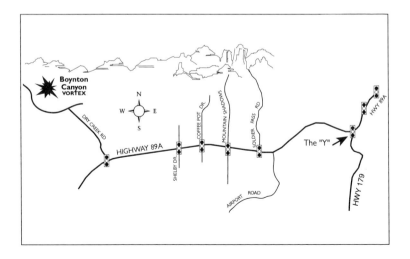

Courthouse Butte Vortex

Located just east of Bell Rock Vortex, this powerful energy center juts up from the earth with great strength and determination.

This vortex site emits an aura of mystery, history and adventure where many travelers claim they have experienced deep spiritual transformations through the entering of portals located within the rock.

Other visitors have described an increased feeling of urgency to complete the unfinished tasks in their lives or to resolve emotional issues they may have been avoiding.

I find this vortex site to be one of the strongest "catalysts" for personal and spiritual growth.

Courthouse Butte

HOW TO GET TO COURTHOUSE BUTTE

Courthouse Butte is the largest rock formation just northeast of Bell Rock. It is located off Hwy 179, just north of the Village of Oak Creek. If you are coming from Sedona, this vortex is just four miles south of the junction of Hwy 89A and Hwy 179 (at the "Y").

There are several turnouts where you may easily park your car in front of Courthouse Butte or Bell Rock. Many visible trailheads will lead you toward this massive formation. There is also an area south of Bell Rock where you can park your car, and though a bit farther to walk, you can easily reach Courthouse Butte.

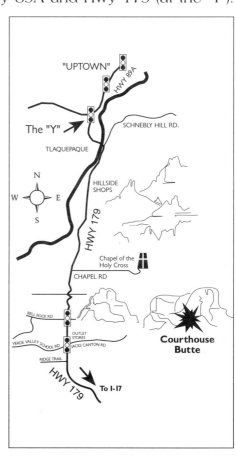

How to Maximize Your Vortex Experience

NOW THAT I'M HERE AT THE VORTEX ... WHAT DO I DO?

Ah! A very important question indeed. After all, you want to get the most out of your Sedona vortex experience now that you've trekked all the way here.

One of the best ways to utilize the energy of the vortex is to meditate. You can also use visualization to enhance your vortex experience and samples of both a meditation and visualization will follow. However, you may also want to find a quiet place off the trail to sit down, close your eyes and relax. Whichever method you choose is correct! There is no prescribed vortex behavior or method that is proven to be the best. It is your individual experience, so create it exactly as you would like it to be. I am now going to give you an example of what I believe to be an effective tool for tapping into and harnessing vortex energy.

During this meditation you can focus on something new that you would like to create in your life or something that you would like to improve upon.

With your eyes closed, focus on breathing in the life-force energy on the vortex while exhaling any fears which may be causing stress in your life. You may also meditate on a personal health issue you would like cleared up, or any intimate relationship in your life you would like to improve. Basically, the choice is yours. Whatever wish or desire you bring to the vortex can be meditated upon to harness the energy.

On the next page is a sample meditation you may want to use once you arrive at your desired location. Remember, this meditation is simply a guide and you may change the wording to personalize it to fit your needs. Relax and have fun!

A Meditation to Maximize Vortex Energy

Meditation

This particular meditation is designed to relieve any physical distress, blockage or disease in the body. Find a comfortable and serene place in the general area of the vortex site where you can sit or lie down.

Now close your eyes and begin to breathe deeply. As you inhale, count to four in your mind slowly and gently as you breathe in the fresh air around you. Exhale, counting to four in the same manner as you focus on releasing any stress, negative thoughts or heavy energy from your body.

Listen to the sounds of nature surrounding you and clear you mind of any other thoughts that may come in. Do not try to fight or force these thoughts out, instead allow them to drift in, acknowledge them and then allow them to float effortlessly out of your mind. The more you are concentrating on the sound of your own breathing, the easier this process will be.

Now begin to relax each part of your body, beginning with your toes. Once your toes are relaxed, move up to your ankles and feel all tension leaving the ankles as they become heavy and sink into the earth beneath you. Next, move up to you calves and feel them relax deeply and become heavy. Continue this process of relaxation for each body part until you reach your head. Do not forget to relax each part of the face... your eyelids, cheeks, forehead, mouth, chin, and tongue.

You should now be in a deeply relaxed meditative state. At this point I would like you to envision your body surrounded in a green mist or cloud of energy. This cloud will hover above you slowly descending with every inhale of your breath until it is lying on top of your body. Breathe this green healing mist into your mouth and nose and feel every pore of your body becoming infused with this energy. Green is the color of healing and will allow you to rejuvenate your body. As you are absorbing the energy, repeat this affirmation in your mind, "It is natural that I am completely healthy and full of vital energy. I release all blocks as vital energy flows freely through my body. I am healthy and so it is."

Now, imagine the powerful energy of the vortex begin to swirl up and infuse your body. This energy will be bright red in color and full of energy. See this swirling mass of red life-force rising up from the earth and fill your body. Repeat the affirmations in your mind as the energy increases. Great job! Keep breathing in counts of four, slowly and gently.

Next, I would like you to imagine a white light coming down from the sky above you. With your eyes still closed, envision this beautiful radiant beam of white energy shining down upon you as you lie on the earth. The light is warm and peaceful, providing you with a feeling of safety, serenity and bliss. As the light shines upon you, feel yourself filling with love and repeat the following in your mind, "I am healed and so it is." Repeat this affirmation eight to ten times.

When you are finished, I would like you to begin to breathe normally and become aware of your surroundings again. Feel the wind blow across your face and hear the sounds of nature all around you. Wiggle your toes as you begin to awaken your body. Now move up to your calves, then your knees and thighs … feeling the energy coming back as each part of your body awakens.

Do this until you reach your head and then slowly open your eyes and take a nice deep cleansing breath.

Congratulations! You have just completed a powerful, healing vortex meditation.

Creative Visualization

A POWERFUL MANIFESTATION TOOL
AT THE VORTEX

Another tool you may find useful for tapping into the vortex energy is VISUALIZATION. Creative visualization is the technique of using your imagination to create what you want in your life. Try not to limit yourself when doing the visualization but instead DREAM BIG! You are in an area that will amplify all you visualize, so be as clear and specific as you can. Most importantly, relax and let go while your imagination takes over. Below is a sample visualization you can tailor to suit your personal needs.

VISUALIZATION

First, try to get into a comfortable position, whether sitting cross-legged on a rock, or lying on your back on a blanket or jacket. Next, close your eyes and begin to become more aware of your breathing as you pull long deep breaths in and slowly release them. Now, think of something you would like to create in your life. It can be a new car, a romantic relationship, increased intuition, or a job promotion. You may also choose something you would like to improve upon, or an event or situation for which you would like a positive and smooth outcome. As you begin to feel more relaxed, start to envision the thing you would like EXACTLY as you would like it. For example, if a new car is your desire, see this new car and choose its color, style, make, and model and visualize yourself behind the steering wheel. Can you smell the new interior of this car? Does it smell like leather? Feel your hands gripping the steering wheel. Is the car a convertible? Is the top down and the warm summer wind blowing through your hair?

Now while holding the image in your mind, mentally make affirmations to yourself that support this vision. "I love my new red convertible sports car!" or, "I own the car of my dreams now, and so it is." Any affirmation will do as long as it supports your image and is stated in a positive manner. Repeat your affirmations eight to ten times and as you do, continue to breathe in and out, remaining as relaxed as possible. When you are finished, slowly open your eyes and begin once again to take note of your surroundings. Sit for a few more minutes while you regain a more conscious and aware state of being. Congratulations! You have just begun to manifest your dreams, utilizing the amazing vortex energy! You may repeat this exercise upon returning home and as often as you would like thereafter.

Testimonials Of Vortex Adventures

SPECTACULAR HEALING EXPERIENCES THAT HAVE OCCURRED AT SEDONA'S VORTEX SITES

I had been feeling restless in my job as an accountant and tired of the mundane existence that had been my life. It was passing me by as I focused on deadlines and bills and all the other stress that had been suffocating me for years. On a trip to Sedona for a vision quest in 1998, I found my spirit that had been lying dormant for so long.

Within the vortices of Boynton Canyon I discovered my true connection with nature and was inspired to follow my long-lost dream of owning a nursery of my own. The energy of this magical land had entered my soul and I became aware for the first time of what really mattered in my life and just how possible my dreams actually were. In this beautiful and sacred land, I became inspired to follow my dreams once and for all.

GEORGE MCCARTHY
Portland, Oregon

*I*n 1984 I visited Sedona for the first time with a friend. We were living in Los Angeles and had no idea of the spiritual power within us or the energetic intensity of Sedona.

We journeyed to Boynton Canyon which was said to be one of the most powerful healing sites in this area. Once there we discovered Mother Kachina Rock. I immediately felt extremely connected to this magical and special tower of red rock. A feeling washed over me that I had found my way home. I stood there for some time in complete awe and inspiration as this feeling enveloped me in warmth and a sense of wholeness. I eventually climbed up to the top where I discovered a small womb-like cave only large enough to barely fit my human frame. My friend advised me to make a wish in this cave ensuring me that the energy of this unique place would make it come true. My wish was clear in that moment ... that I must come here to live in Sedona, this amazing place of beauty and nature. This wish was made in August of 1994 and I moved to Sedona in November of the same year.

SAN DAN YI
World Renowned Healer & Teacher - Sedona, AZ

*A*t the Cathedral Rock Vortex I felt the deepest sense of peace and serenity—a feeling I had not been able to find in years. I work in a high stress sales job and have four kids at home. The peace and physical rejuvenation that I received in just an hour at the vortex was enough to renew my spirit and vitality at home for the next year!

ANNE HELLER
Sante Fe, New Mexico

Twelve years ago I had some kind of inner calling. I had never heard of Sedona or of its intense Vortex energy.

Living for the past 20 years in California at the time and working in corporate America, I knew I had to make an escape. I quit my job, sold everything I owned and crammed what was left into the car with my husband. We headed to Colorado stopping along the way in towns and cities that had no appeal to me. Arriving in Colorado, we were once again disappointed. Sure it was beautiful but it just didn't feel 'special.' We turned around at that point and headed for home.

"On the way we decided to go through Flagstaff, Arizona where we met a woman who told us we must take the scenic drive down Oak Creek Canyon. As we neared the bottom of the canyon and entered the area known as Sedona, I was breathless. I felt such overwhelming joy and bliss and a connection with nature, Mother Earth and all living things that I could not speak for the next hour. I knew in an instant that nothing else up to that point mattered. My old job, the money, the new Cadillac, the house on the ocean ... it was all irrelevant. I was later to find out that this Canyon was a vortex of spiritual energy.

Later that day, we "coincidentally" ran into someone we knew from California who was now living in Sedona. During that conversation my husband was offered a job in Sedona with free housing and living expenses! The experience I had just had in the canyon was so profound and then in the next moment, Sedona was being offered to us as a new home ... a gift from Spirit.

A few months later, we were living here in Sedona and it was a move that forever changed my life. I have met many more travelers with stories about Sedona's magic just like mine.

LINDA COLLINS
Chicago, IL

*O*ne summer day last September I visited Bell Rock to meet some friends and partake in a meditation ceremony. I stepped out of my car and felt my usual reaction to the awesome energy of Bell Rock. I had visited this site before and had always had this immediate energetic reaction as the hair on my arms and neck stood up and I could feel intense energy reverberating throughout my entire body.

I had planned on meeting friends there but they were running late so I headed up the rock at dusk with only my blanket underarm, having forgotten my flashlight.

Near the top of the vortex the sky became darker and I suddenly felt lost in my surroundings, unable to see ahead of me, let alone find my way back down the path. After a momentary sense of panic, I felt a voice inside of me telling me to stand still and not to try and get down but to stay put and I would be safe. This voice was nurturing and seemed to be coming from within Bell Rock. An immediate sense of calm came over me as the voice further instructed me that if I needed to sleep right in this very spot on the rock, I would be completely taken care of and free of any danger.

I stood in that moment feeling overwhelming peace and serenity to the core of my being. I feel that this voice was the rock speaking to me and telling me to trust and that I would be protected—a message that was meant to be applied to my entire life at that time.

After standing for what seemed like an hour in that dark but safe place, my friends finally arrived with their flashlights to help me down. Now in the light, I discovered that I had been on the edge of a drop-off and could have been seriously hurt had I not stayed still and listened to the voice.

Once we arrived at a safe place near the base of the rock, we began our meditation as planned. During this meditation I was told by the facilitator to put my forehead down on the rock to receive my message. At this point I once again heard a clear and distinct voice telling me that everything would be okay but that I needed to take care of myself more in my life and to honor Mother Earth on my spiritual journey.

This message made sense to me considering where I was currently at in my life since I was taking care of a sacred piece of land and had been practicing and studying Native American Spirituality.

I believe that the energy of Bell Rock and the voice within the vortex had contacted me with a personal spiritual mes-

sage for my life that I have never forgotten, and which was just the beginning of many more of these 'guided experiences' to come.

MARCIA KOWAL
Sedona, Arizona

*A*irport Mesa Vortex hit me like a jolt of electricity! Originally from Greece, I was in awe of the beauty of Sedona at first glance. I had never encountered landscape and scenery so unusually beautiful in my entire life and travels around the world.*

When I ventured up to Airport Mesa with some friends I immediately felt as if I had been 'plugged in' to an incredible outlet of pure energy. I had to leave the group and venture off on my own because the energy was so powerful.

Once I found an area to sit down on the Earth, I could literally feel my physical body being regenerated and rejuvenated. I had a kundalini-rising experience right then and there and I am certain that this energy cleared and opened up all of my chakras. This energy renewal stayed with me for months following and I continue to have the same experience each time I visit the Airport Vortex.

ZEFFIE KAFALA
Sedona, AZ

*I*n February of 1995 we had just opened our new Healing Center in Sedona. We received a call from the Oprah Winfrey show saying that they were doing a show on famous cities and what they are known for. They had chosen Sedona because of the Vortex energy and alternative types of healing experiences that many practice here and have experienced over the years.

On the day of the show taping we all stood around waiting breathlessly for Oprah's arrival. However, we instead greeted a member of her staff who had been sent to receive a healing and psychic experience that she could then relay back to the show staff. This woman was definitely skeptical but agreed to stay in Sedona for three days of 'metaphysical experiences.'

We sent one of our psychic readers with her to act as her guide. Our guide took the woman to Bell Rock, Cathedral Rock and Boynton Canyon and they immediately said they felt an energy there that left them feeling uplifted and physically regenerated.

The skepticism of this woman and her camera crew began fading as our psychic gave them readings at the vortex sites that were remarkably accurate. They also performed healings on the crew at the Vortex sites and asked for feedback as to what the clients had felt. All reported a feeling of increased physical energy and a deep sense of inner peace and serenity. The Oprah crew began asking many questions and were eager to learn more about this new energy they had tapped into. These so-called skeptics suddenly could not wait to experience the Vortex energy again.

Since this experience in 1995, the woman from the Oprah show has been in touch several times and has written to thank us for an experience that she claims has "opened up the door to her spirituality and set her on the path to enlightenment." She claims that the energy she tapped into at the Vortices in Sedona stayed with her when she returned home and inspired her to pursue many spiritual avenues in her life that she may not have prior to her trip to Sedona.

The best thing about this story is that it is only one of the many hundreds of testimonials we've received from people affected by the powerful energy of this sacred land that has helped to redefine and open up fascinating and magical doors of healing in their lives.

ANITA DALTON
Sedona, Arizona

*W*hen I first began visiting Cathedral Rock Vortex, I found a crevice at the site that I kept being drawn to. I had tried to climb to this area but could not seem to reach it by foot. Finally, a friend of mine said he could take me up there by climbing up the other side of the rock formation—a very treacherous trail that had me quite afraid.

When we reached the area we found that we were still 20 feet beneath the crevice and could not proceed any further.

We decided to meditate on a knoll below the crevice. As we were meditating, I went into a deep trance state. Suddenly I sensed a being or presence behind me that ethereally placed a glowing necklace around my neck. I immediately knew this was some type of key that was to allow me access into the above crevice where I could enter a portal.

In the next instant I was inside the crevice and had entered this portal. On the wall in front of me water dripped from the rock and into a stone bowl beneath it. I knew I was to wash my hands in this bowl and I also intuitively sensed another being to the right of me who was showing me what to do. I then stepped to my right to an opening where light was emanating and glowing. In this opening was a cylindrical crystal cave that was illuminated with colors of the rainbow bouncing off of all of the crystals that lined this cave.

I had been floating this whole time amongst all of this light and beauty, knowing that I could fly high up into the universe if I wanted or deep into the core of the Earth. The sensation was that there was no limitation and the message was clear that I could revisit this portal at any time in the future and would never need to climb again to the area to do so. In the next instant, I was sitting back on the knoll filled with a deep peace and serenity. I knew that I had just been given a great gift that I could access at any time.

RUTHIE FERRONE
Sedona, Arizona

Your Journey Has Only Begun

You do not have to visit the vortex sites on your own. For those interested in a vortex tour, Sedona offers many. You may decide on a personal guided tour or a group jeep vortex tour. I have found the personal spiritual tours to be the most beneficial.

When you choose a special tour you are able to visit each vortex for longer periods of time and most will include a guided meditation or ritual ceremony. You also have the opportunity to have individual attention from the guide and a more personalized tour tailored to meet your specific needs and requests. For this reason, a personally guided tour allows you and your party to reap the most benefit from these powerful energy centers.

If you choose a jeep tour you will have the opportunity to meet other travelers from all over the world and will be free of any hiking as you are safely driven to the most well-known sites. On these tours you will want to pack a light jacket as the rides in the morning and early evening can get chilly! Become unlimited as you embark on your adventure to Sedona's gateways of energy! Have fun, be safe and let the magical journey begin.

Other Attractions to See While in Sedona

So here you are visiting the beautiful town of Sedona and would like to know where the locals go to hang out in the red rocks, get a bite to eat, or do their shopping. We have compiled a list of all the best places to go and "must see" locations below. Enjoy, have fun, and ignore your watch for a day as you surrender to the spontaneity and fun of this remarkable place.

Places to See

Palatki Ruins

These ancient cliff dwellings are located in the Boynton Canyon area in a box canyon off Red Canyon. This sacred site has been known to evoke past-life memories and events for many who have visited. It is said that these ruins were occupied by the Native Americans from 1150 to 1250 A.D. There are no records thus far as to why this land was vacated, however, there are various theories. Visit the Palatki Ruins for yourself and see what clues you can come up with. You may be able to come up with your own theories and ideas as to who these ancient people were and why they vanished. (See photo pg 14.)

Devil's Bridge

This natural landmark formed out of sandstone is a must-see and well worth the mini-hike. Located approximately 3 miles west of Sedona at Grasshopper Flats, you will find the end of Dry Creek Road where it turns into a dirt trail. Follow this until it branches and stay towards the right when the trail forks and heads into Sterling Canyon where you cannot miss Devil's Bridge.

Vultee Arch

If you continue to follow the path from Devil's Bridge until it ends, you will find yourself at the trailhead for Vultee Arch. Continue down the trail for 3.5 miles to view this amazing red rock arch located 400 feet above the starting point.

Places to Eat

Red Planet Diner

For inexpensive, great tasting food with the best atmosphere—this is the place. The expansive menu includes treats for the little ones, such as hamburgers and milkshakes, and Italian cuisine such as the Chicken Parmigiana for the more discriminating palate. The prices are reasonable, the food is consistent and filling and the atmosphere—out of this world as you dine beneath the Solar System and UFOs. The diner is always busy so arrive with the early lunch crowd at 11:00 am or the early dinner crowd at 5:00 pm to avoid the rush! They are open until 11:00 pm every evening. 1655 West Hwy 89A in Sedona.

Dahl & Diluca Restorante Italiano

For fine Italian dining in the middle of the desert, this is the place. As you step through the doors, you are transported to an Italian village of great beauty and aromatic smells. Since the owner is also the chef, each dish is prepared with care and pride. Nightly music adds to the ambiance of your Italian adventure. Dinner is served from 5:00 to 9:00 pm. Reservations recommended. 2321 West Hwy 89A, Sedona.

Bagel Talk

For a quick breakfast or a prepared lunch to take with you on the Vortex trails, you can't beat these chewy bagels. Many flavors to choose from as well as assorted cream cheeses and Boar's Head Deli Meats for sandwiches. Opens early in the morning at 7:00 am with fresh brewed coffee and warm bagels. 30 Bell Rock Plaza (Village of Oak Creek).

Places to Get Your Supplies

Center For the New Age

This is your one-stop metaphysical shop with everything from crystals, books and jewelry to candles, sage and other ritual aids. Sedona's largest new age store, the Center for the New Age also features 20 psychic readers and healers on-site as well as astrology reports and aura photos. Stop in and mention this book for your free gift. 341 Hwy 179 Sedona (Across from Tlaquepaque)

Bike and Bean

For your biking needs, you can get it all in one stop where trained professionals can assist you with mountain bike rentals, trail maps and advice, safety equipment and repairs, as well as a fresh cup of coffee. 6020 Hwy 179 in Sedona.

About the Author

Jamie Jones is an aura photographer and reader. She has used biofeedback imaging to photograph and interpret the human energy fields of thousands, assisting them in healing and personal spiritual growth. In doing this work, Jamie has been able to utilize the energy of Sedona's Vortex sites to further increase the healing process of her many clients and to capture this progress on film via aura photography.

Jamie's other passion includes swimming with dolphins in the wild. She has led dolphin swim tours to share the magical healing experience of these amazing beings.